SIEGE OF MALTA 1940–42

In memory of George Dale

IMAGES OF WAR

SIEGE OF MALTA 1940–42

RARE PHOTOGRAPHS FROM VETERANS' COLLECTIONS

Anthony Rogers

Greenhill Books

First published in Great Britain in 2020 by

Greenhill Books

c/o Pen & Sword Books Ltd, 47 Church Street, Barnsley,
South Yorkshire, S70 2AS, England
For more information on our books, please visit
www.greenhillbooks.com, email contact@greenhillbooks.com
or write to us at the above address.

ISBN 978-1-78438-459-3

A CIP catalogue record for this book is available from the British Library.

Typeset in Gill Sans by Concept, Huddersfield, West Yorkshire, HD4 5JL
Printed and bound in Malta by Gutenberg Press

Contents

Image Sources

In the Second World War, and wars since, whoever possessed a camera almost always shared the same prints among friends. Malta was no exception. There are countless photographs of Malta during the Second World War. They were taken by official military and press photographers, as well as by ordinary British servicemen. The latter were required to obtain a permit to own and use a camera in wartime and then adhere to strict guidelines. Some did, some didn't. Amateur snaps often lack the finesse of a professional photograph, but can be all the more interesting in portraying the true nature of war: the camaraderie, the routine and, sometimes, the action. The majority of images reproduced here originally belonged to those who survived the siege of Malta. Without their kind help and generosity this book would not have been possible.

Introduction

In 1814 Malta joined the British Empire, serving as an outpost for the Royal Navy and the British Army and, more than a century later, the Royal Air Force (RAF). Throughout history, Malta had provided a succession of rulers with an ideal military base, strategically situated in the middle of the Mediterranean, almost equidistant from Gibraltar to the west and Alexandria, Egypt, to the east. At 17½ miles by 8¼, it is the largest of the Maltese Islands. Gozo and Comino are just to the north. Other, uninhabited, islets complete the archipelago.

Being connected to Britain could be advantageous, but when, on 10 June 1940, Italy joined with Germany in the war against Britain and France, for Malta and, to a lesser degree, Gozo, the implications were very serious. The Maltese Islands were within easy reach of the Sicily-based bombers and fighters of the Regia Aeronautica (Italian air force) and as a Crown Colony, Malta in particular was now a prime Axis target. To counter the threat, there were thirty-four heavy anti-aircraft (HAA) guns, eight Bofors light anti-aircraft (LAA) guns and a number of coast guns, as well as twenty-four searchlights. There was also a radio direction finder station (in July it would be joined by a second RDF unit). The island's main aerodrome, near Luqa village, was not yet fully operational. But, then, there was no fighter defence as such, other than a few Royal Navy Gloster Sea Gladiators recently taken over by the RAF.

Following Italy's declaration of war in June 1940, Malta became a prime target of the Regia Aeronautica. The Italians were joined, in January 1941, by units of the Luftwaffe (German air force).

Notwithstanding Italo-German efforts to neutralise Malta, the island was still able to provide the Royal Navy with a base from which to strike at Axis shipping, thus creating a constant drain on the enemy's Mediterranean supply routes and presenting a serious problem for Axis forces in Libya. In June 1940 Malta's Gladiators had been joined by five Hawker Hurricanes, which were retained after landing at the island while en route to the Middle East. Maintaining the island's fighter force was to fall mainly on the Royal Navy. By the end of June the following year, aircraft carriers had ferried more than 200 Hurricanes to within flying range of Malta. Most arrived safely. Some were allocated for the island's defence; others continued to the Western Desert. In addition to fighters, Malta also provided facilities for other aircraft types, with pilots and aircrew of both the RAF and Fleet Air Arm (FAA) undertaking offensive and reconnaissance missions.

In mid-1941 the balance of air power shifted between opposing sides in the central Mediterranean. German resources were required for the imminent German invasion of Russia. In May German bombers began to be redeployed from Sicily. The war in the Western Desert also had to be considered and in June would result in the withdrawal from Sicily of Messerschmitt Bf109s. For a few months the RAF would again have only the Regia Aeronautica to contend with.

There was a sharp decline in Italian aerial activity during August and September 1941. For the first time, Malta's forces were able to meet the enemy on a more equal footing, with the Royal Navy and Merchant Navy delivering, between July and September, twenty-two Hurricanes and seven Swordfish in addition to personnel and thousands of tons of supplies. The Italians did what they could to disrupt operations, but of fifteen cargo ships and other vessels that made up the convoys 'Substance' and 'Halberd' in July and September, just two ships were sunk. October and November saw the arrival of more aircraft, including thirty-four Hurricanes. But the Royal Navy suffered a major loss when HMS *Ark Royal* was torpedoed and sunk by the German submarine *U-81*. All but one of the crew were saved.

With the approach of winter, the Luftwaffe again began to wind down operations on the Eastern Front and Adolf Hitler once more turned his attention to the Mediterranean and Malta in particular.

In order to survive, Malta continued to be resupplied by sea. Foodstuffs and all manner of materiel had been delivered but the number of fighters received so far was insufficient. On 7 March 1942 fifteen Spitfire Mk VBs were flown in from HMS *Eagle*. The Spitfire was to make a distinct impression on the air battle. The Mk V was a fighter with a speed to match the Bf109 and the firepower required to destroy the Ju88.

In March Generalfeldmarschall Kesselring announced a new strategy with the aim of destroying the RAF fighters on the ground prior to dealing with any remaining bombers and torpedo aircraft and then concentrating on targets in the area of Grand Harbour. In the evening of 20 March a powerful force, including approximately fifty Ju88s, opened the new phase by hitting Ta' Qali. The destruction was such that the aerodrome was rendered temporarily unserviceable. Bombs also fell well outside the target area, killing and injuring civilians.

II. Fliegerkorps was relentless in its efforts to pound Malta into submission. Ongoing Spitfire deliveries and Hurricane reinforcements were barely sufficient to sustain an effective fighter force. But Malta held out. The unwavering decision of the Maltese to stand fast with Britain was formally recognised on 15 April 1942 by King George VI: 'To honour her brave people I award the George Cross to the Island Fortress of Malta to bear witness to a heroism and devotion that will long be famous in history.' It was the highest honour that an appreciative British sovereign could bestow on a community.

In late April Allied reconnaissance aircraft photographed what appeared to be three airfields under construction in Sicily. All indications were that they were intended for gliders for an Axis invasion of Malta. Codenamed 'Herkules' by the Germans and 'C3' by the Italians, such an operation had indeed been planned for that summer, with an attack force five times the strength of that deployed during the 1941 German invasion of Crete. But 'Herkules' would never materialise, with Hitler instead giving priority to offensives in Russia and North Africa. Ultimately, the German *Afrikakorps* would be fought to a standstill, thereby shifting the balance of military power in the central Mediterranean. But for all on Malta in April 1942, the threat of invasion was very real and would remain so for months to come.

By the end of the month a significant reduction in Sicily-based Luftwaffe units was under way, as bombers and fighters were again redeployed. Attacks against Malta would continue, but on a lesser scale, and supplemented by Italian aircraft. The latest Luftwaffe offensive was wound down at a critical time. Such had been its effect that the 10th Submarine Flotilla now departed Malta for the safety of Alexandria. The submarines would not return until the end of July.

According to Luftwaffe records, Malta operations between 20 March and 28 April 1942 involved 5,807 sorties by bombers, 5,667 by fighters and 345 by reconnaissance aircraft — a total of 11,819 sorties. In this five-and-a-half-week period the weight of bombs dropped is reported to have exceeded 6,557 tonnes.

Early on 9 May, 650 miles west of Malta, the carriers HMS *Eagle* and USS *Wasp* flew off sixty-four Spitfires, fifty-nine of which arrived safely. The Luftwaffe and the Regia Aeronautica were determined to destroy the new arrivals. But after two days of intense aerial activity, it seemed that Malta's Spitfires had gained the initiative. Although there would be several more months of hard fighting before the siege was finally raised, 10 May 1942 is considered a turning point in a battle that had already lasted nearly two years.

In the latter half of May German fighter strength was further reduced, leaving *Stab* and *II. Gruppe* of *Jagdgeschwader 53* in Sicily, together with a number of bombers and other aircraft types. Operations were undertaken mainly by Italians, but lacked the tenacity of German sorties. As had occurred in mid-1941, therefore, Malta took the opportunity to reorganise and at the same time improve its position, not least with a substantial increase in offensive and defensive aircraft. Fighters were a priority and on 18 May HMS *Eagle* ferried to the island seventeen more Spitfires. On 3 June thirty-one Spitfires took off from HMS *Eagle*; all but four reached Malta. Just six days later the carrier delivered another thirty-two, nearly all of which landed without mishap. The Spitfire had now replaced the Hurricane altogether in defending Malta's skies.

July began with a renewed Axis offensive that would continue for the next two weeks. RAF losses were alleviated when HMS *Eagle* delivered thirty-one Spitfires on 15 July followed, on the 21st, by twenty-eight more.

The Spitfire was pivotal to the defence of Malta. But the overall situation remained critical. In order to survive, Malta needed a constant resupply of aviation fuel, ammunition and other essentials. Operation 'Pedestal', launched in August 1942, resulted in the delivery of around 32,000 tons of supplies, as well as thirty-seven Spitfires, but at a heavy cost in lives and materiel.

There had been a noticeable decline in enemy air activity, but the Axis Command was still very much concerned about the ongoing disruption to Rommel's Mediterranean supply routes and by October the Luftwaffe had again gathered in Sicily a formidable force. On 11 October the Germans and their Italian allies launched the first in a series of attacks in a concerted effort to crush Malta. This, the final Axis offensive, would continue for one week. Axis efforts to subjugate Malta were greatly diminished by November.

Following a successful Allied offensive at El Alamein in Egypt, Anglo-American forces landed in French North Africa on 8 November. For Malta the main problem continued to be one of provisions, with individual ships and submarines assisting with supply runs. It was not until 20 November 1942 that the siege was finally lifted with the arrival during Operation 'Stoneage' of all four merchantmen: the Dutch *Bantam*, British *Denbighshire*, and American *Mormacmoon* and *Robin Locksley*.

The Battle of Britain being one notable exception, the first three years of war had not gone well for British and Commonwealth forces. The Wehrmacht had overrun much of Europe before turning on Russia. Japan had made important gains in east and south-east Asia, and while American forces were by this time engaged in the Pacific, they had yet to make an impression in North Africa and Europe. In the central Mediterranean, however, there had at last been a significant turn of events: against the odds, Malta had held out against a sustained Axis air campaign and emerged triumphant.

The Central Mediterranean. From June 1940 until mid-1943 Sicily and Italy remained Axis territory. At the same time Allied and Axis forces battled for control of North Africa. In-between the British-held Maltese Islands dominated central Mediterranean shipping routes.

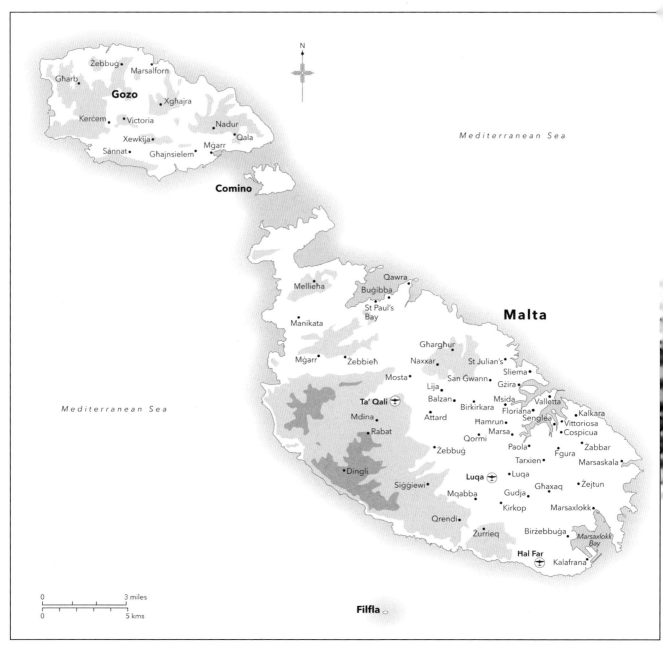

The Maltese Islands. The coastlines of Malta and Gozo have changed slightly since the 1940s. This map shows the islands as they are today. There is now a port facility at what was Kalafrana seaplane base. The Dockyard area has also undergone reconstruction. There is a ferry terminal at Marfa in northern Malta, and at Gozo the port of Mġarr has been modernised. Of the aerodromes that were operational during the period 1940–42, Luqa is still in use as the island's airport.

Chapter One

Island Fortress

On 11 June 1940, when Italy commenced hostilities against Malta, the island's fighter defence was reliant on four ex-Royal Navy Gloster Sea Gladiators. These biplanes were taken over by the RAF and flown by pilots with no prior combat experience. When one machine was written off, another would be brought out of storage.

(**Opposite, above**) Six Gladiators are known to have been on strength at various times. After the first two days of war, however, it seems that no more than three such aircraft were seen in the air at any one time. Someone – it is not known who or when – immortalised Malta's Gladiators as 'Faith', 'Hope' and 'Charity'. Here are N5520, N5524 and N5529 at Luqa aerodrome in the late summer or autumn of 1940. N5520 was still in use, albeit for meteorological flights, in February 1942, before being written off in a landing accident at Ħal Far aerodrome. The fuselage was removed to a nearby field, from where it was recovered and in 1943 put on display as 'Faith'. In the 1970s it was partially restored by RAF volunteers and is today an exhibit at Malta's War Museum.

(**Opposite, below**) Although lacking fighters, Malta was unique in having been equipped with the first RDF unit outside the United Kingdom. Other Air Ministry Experimental Stations would arrive in due course.

Rooftop view of a typical village or small town. Clouds of smoke and dust from exploding bombs can be seen in the distance.

For some Maltese, such as this dapper barman, the war was more or less business as usual, at least initially. This is thought to be 'Tony's Bar', either in Valletta or Sliema.

British servicemen could be posted to Malta for years and inevitably romances developed with local ladies. This is the wedding day of RAF Sergeant Robert V. Gridley. Like many in wartime, this marriage was short-lived. On 13 January 1942, Gridley, by this time a Pilot Officer, was an air gunner in a 69 Squadron Maryland when it was attacked by Messerschmitt Bf 109s and shot down off Malta's coast. The observer, Pilot Officer Arnold Potter baled out. The pilot, Wing Commander John N. Dowland GC, and Bob Gridley died. John Dowland's body was apparently recovered for burial at Malta. Bob Gridley has no known grave.

(**Opposite, above**) Expatriate British children relaxing with senior non-commissioned officer fighter pilots and aircrew at an unidentified location in mid-1940. Among those shown are James Pickering (*standing*), P.D.J. 'Paddy' Moren (*sitting, left*) and, to his left, W.J. (Bill) Timms, Frank Bastard and Bob Gridley.

(**Opposite, below**) Those too young to serve in the armed forces often volunteered for other tasks. The Malta Auxiliary Corps (MAC) was formed before the outbreak of war and supplemented army units with general duties personnel. During the siege they assisted at gun batteries and other hazardous locations. Many teenagers served in the MAC, including two of the author's uncles, seen here with a sister and her daughter at their home village of Żurrieq.

(**Above**) The first siege of Malta took place in 1565 and, after a four-month battle, ended in defeat for the Ottoman invading force. When the fighting was over, a new capital city, Valletta, was constructed on former Turkish positions along a high promontory. It is bordered on three sides by the sea, with a deep defensive ditch on the landward side. Nearly 400 years later Malta was again besieged, but by a very different foe. The island's limestone structure, however, favoured the defenders. Buildings were (and still are) constructed almost entirely of limestone blocks. Such buildings could be destroyed by bombing, but they would not catch fire. Incendiary devices, therefore, were all but redundant. Limestone, relatively soft when quarried, hardens when exposed to the elements. It is therefore easy to tunnel into. Numerous air raid shelters were hewn out of the solid rock below Valletta's walls and at many other locations. Some civilians who had been bombed out of their homes took up temporary accommodation in such places. Conditions were far from ideal, but at least provided a degree of safety.

(**Opposite, above**) In a Maltese field a soldier sifts through the wreckage of a crashed aircraft. During the battle for Malta more than a thousand British, Italian and German aircraft were lost.

(**Opposite, below**) During air raids, bombs often missed the target to fall in neighbouring residential areas. Malta was and largely still is Roman Catholic and so it was especially tragic for parishioners when their church was damaged or destroyed. This is the Church of Sant' Andrija (St Andrew's) at Luqa village.

(**Above**) Malta would endure nearly two and a half years of air raids, with more than 3,000 alerts before the war was over. As the island's main port, Grand Harbour was vital to Malta's survival but by the end of 1942 it was a scene of destruction. In this poignant photo, a serviceman gazes at a merchantman moored in Dockyard Creek.

In 1940 General John Standish Surtees Prendergast Vereker VC commanded the British Expeditionary Force in France. Lord Gort, as he was generally known, went on to become aide-de-camp to King George VI and Governor and Commander-in-Chief of Gibraltar. In May 1942 he succeeded General Sir William Dobbie as Governor and Commander-in-Chief of Malta.

Chapter Two

The Air War: 1940

At dawn on 11 June 1940 *2ª Squadra Aerea* of the Regia Aeronautica commenced operations against Malta. Macchi C.200 fighters accompanied the first Savoia-Marchetti S.79 bombers across the 50 miles of sea that separate the Maltese Islands from Sicily. Three Gladiators intercepted the raiders in this, the first of countless aerial engagements during the next two-and-a-half years. By day's end, all Italian aircraft had returned to base; just one enemy airman had been wounded. The majority of the Allied casualties were Maltese, both military and civilian, including several who were killed when three naval launches off Malta's Grand Harbour were misidentified and sunk by shore defences.

(**Opposite, above**) In the morning of 10 July 1940 some twenty S.79s attacked the Dockyard area, Manoel Island, Tarxien and Żabbar. Hurricanes of Malta's Fighter Flight intercepted the raiders and two S.79s were destroyed. One was shot down by Flying Officer William 'Timber' Woods and crashed offshore. Flying Officer Frederic F. Taylor attacked the other. This, the first enemy aircraft to fall on Maltese soil, came down in flames just behind the seventeenth century De Redin Tower east of Fort San Leonardo, damaging nearby Post RA6, which was occupied by personnel of B Company, 1st Battalion The Dorsetshire Regiment. Three soldiers suffered extensive burns (two died two days later). One airman baled out of the stricken *195ª Squadriglia B.T.* machine, only for his parachute to catch fire. Neither he, nor any of those from either of the shot-down aircraft, survived.

(**Opposite, below**) A tri-motor S.79 of *36° Stormo B.T.* at Castelvetrano, Sicily, after returning with battle damage from a mission to Malta.

(**Above**) Operation 'Hurry' was the first attempt to reinforce Malta with fighters from an aircraft carrier. This photograph was taken on board HMS *Argus* at Gibraltar in July 1940. The sergeant pilot in shirt-sleeves is thought to be Roy O'Donnell, who was shot down and killed just two weeks after this picture was taken. To his right is Sergeant Bill Timms, who lost his life as a result of a low-level bale-out from his Hurricane on 11 January 1941.

(**Opposite, above**) At dawn on 2 August 1940 twelve Hurricane Mk Is of 418 Flight took off from *Argus* to fly to Malta, a distance of 380 miles. At Luqa they would join surviving fighters to form 261 Squadron.

(**Opposite, below**) At Luqa aerodrome in the summer of 1940 fighter pilots of the recently formed 261 Squadron wait at dispersal, a modified bus. Sergeant Oswald R. 'Drac' Bowerman (*left*) is playing chess with Sergeant Dennis K. Ashton. In the background is Sergeant Eric N. Kelsey. All three would be dead before the end of 1942.

Sergeant Eric Kelsey arrived at Malta during Operation 'Hurry'. He is seen here in an apparently unguarded moment, and (**opposite, above**) with a Gladiator at Luqa aerodrome. Kelsey failed to return from a sortie on 19 January 1941.

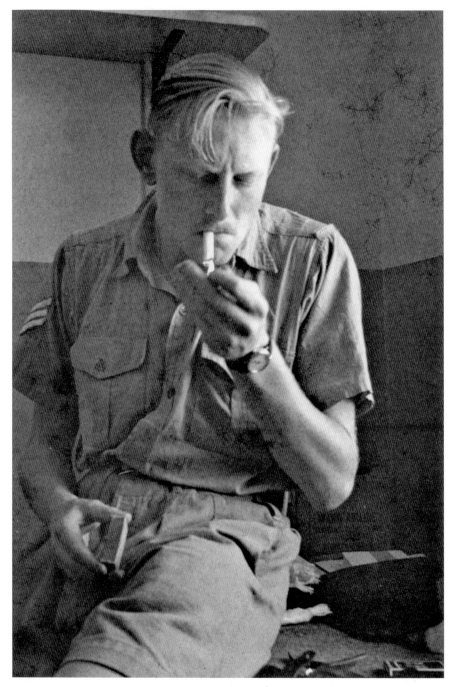

(**Opposite, above**) By the end of June 1940 Malta's Gladiators had been joined by five Hurricanes. When flown by a proficient pilot, the Hurricane was more than capable of dealing with whatever the Italian air force could deploy at this stage of the war. This, one of the first official photographs of Hurricanes at Malta, shows a sergeant pilot of 261 Squadron just returned from a sortie.

D 526-L.C.Castelvetrano 22-11-40

(**Opposite, above**) A Hurricane landing at Luqa. This appears to be N2622, from which Sergeant Bill Timms baled out and was killed on 11 January 1941.

(**Opposite, below**) Countless aircraft of all types were damaged or written off in take-off and landing accidents, such as this Wellington at Luqa aerodrome in 1940.

(**Above**) S.79 at Castelvetrano in November 1940.

Postcard dropped by the Regia Aeronautica on Ta' Qali aerodrome, c. November 1940. The Regia Aeronautica had been quite unable to wear down Malta's defences and such bravado only served to amuse Malta's fighter pilots. But the situation was about to change.

Chapter Three

The Air War: 1941

Mussolini's offensive against Malta and the British Mediterranean Fleet, combined with the North African campaign and Italy's invasion of Greece, finally led Hitler to reinforce his ally in the Mediterranean. Towards the end of 1940 elements of *X. Fliegerkorps* of the Luftwaffe, commanded by Generalleutnant Hans-Ferdinand Geisler, began to arrive in Sicily from Norway. By mid-January 1941 the Luftwaffe had gathered in Sicily a formidable array of front-line aircraft that included Ju 87s and 88s, Heinkel He 111s and Messerschmitt Bf 110s.

(**Opposite, above**) The Luftwaffe commenced operations against Malta in January 1941. The arrival at Grand Harbour of the battle-damaged carrier HMS *Illustrious* on 10 January resulted in heavy raids on the Dockyard area. Enemy aircraft were engaged by anti-aircraft (AA) gunners and fighter pilots of 261 Squadron. This is one of a series of images of what became known as 'the Illustrious Blitz' taken by a since-forgotten photographer from a vantage point overlooking Grand Harbour. *Illustrious* is visible underneath the floating crane on the right.

(**Opposite, below**) A single S.79 escorted by several Fiat CR.42s appeared over the north coast of Malta in the late morning of 1 February. AA guns and RAF fighters engaged. Sergeant Frederick N. Robertson shot down a CR.42. The biplane crashed on farmland just across the main road, south-west of St Andrew's Barracks. The pilot, Sergente Andrea Baudoni of *379ª Squadriglia C.T.*, was killed.

Sergeant Fred Robertson, pictured after being awarded the Distinguished Flying Medal in March 1941. Later commissioned, Flying Officer Robertson was one of eleven men killed in an aircraft collision on 31 August 1943.

In this undated image, bombs explode on Ħal Far aerodrome as a Ju 88 of *I.Gruppe* of *Kampfgeschwader 54* flies along the south coast. *K.G.54* was one of the first German bomber units to operate over Malta in early 1941.

(**Above**) In February 1941 Bf109 Es of *7.Staffel* of *Jagdgeschwader 26* were transferred from Germany south to Gela, in Sicily. The outstanding *Staffelkapitän* was Oberleutnant Joachim Müncheberg, credited with twenty-three 'kills', and a recipient of the coveted *Ritterkreuz* (Knight's Cross). The faster, cannon-armed Bf109 was more than a match for Malta's Hurricanes. In four months the fighter pilots of *7./J.G.26* would claim at least forty-two air victories (including two during the unit's brief involvement in the invasion of Yugoslavia); twenty of these were credited to Müncheberg. Incredibly, not one Messerschmitt was lost over Malta. On 12 February *7./J.G.26* escorted bombers of *III./Lehrgeschwader* 1 to Malta. It was the first time German fighters had appeared over the island. This unique image is a record of that occasion. 'White 11' is in the foreground, with 'White 10' on its right.

(**Opposite, above**) For *7./J.G.26* and *III./L.G.1* the raid on 12 February 1941 was a complete success. *Ritter-kreuzträger* Oberleutnant Gerhard Richter (*centre, facing left*) had further cause to celebrate, having also completed his 100th mission. Richter served in the post-war Bundeswehr, eventually retiring as Oberstleutnant.

(**Opposite, below**) A Ju88 of *III./L.G.1* off the south coast of Malta.

At the end of October 1940 headquarters and maintenance staff from RAF Luqa were dispatched to a civil aerodrome overlooked by the ancient city of Mdina, in an area known locally as Ta' Qali. On 8 November this became Royal Air Force Station Ta Kali and the new base for 261 Squadron. This is the orderly room sergeant at Ta' Qali in early 1941. On the landing ground behind can be seen a Gladiator and a Hurricane. Note the Imperial Airways bell. Imperial Airways, British Airways and Italy's Ala Littoria all used the aerodrome before it was closed to civil airlines at the end of January 1940. Ala Littoria relocated to Hal Far and on 29 January joined the two British airlines at Luqa. (Incredibly, there were no objections by the Air Ministry when Ala Littoria requested a plan of Luqa aerodrome.)

(**Opposite**) During a raid on 26 February 1941 Luqa aerodrome was severely damaged and at least six Wellingtons were destroyed. Ju 87 5718/6G+PR was one of two Stukas down just close to the aerodrome. Feldwebel Johannes Braun and his wireless operator, Feldwebel Justin Kästle, lost their lives. Among those photographed at the crash site was Bombardier George Dale of 10th HAA Regiment.

RAF personnel pose with a Hurricane shortly after relocating from Luqa to Ta' Qali. The pristine condition of this aircraft is indicative of a recent arrival.

Ta' Qali, early 1941: 261 Squadron fighter pilots on stand-by await the order to scramble.

Flying Officer Gerald H. Bellamy in early 1941, soon after joining 261 Squadron. He would survive the war.

(**Above**) Included in spite of being slightly out of focus, is this rare image of a Hurricane of 261 Squadron against a typical Maltese landscape.

(**Right**) Sergeant John K. Norwell in 261 Squadron's stand-by bus. 'Angus' Norwell was later commissioned and retired from the RAF after the war.

(**Opposite, above**) The 'Mad House' (Chateau Bertrand) was a distinctive building at Ta' Qali. It was taken over by the RAF but later demolished after having been severely damaged by bombing.

(**Opposite, below**) On 10 March low-flying aircraft, probably Messerschmitt Bf 110s, strafed St Paul's Bay. Sunderland T9046 was shot up and damaged and Sunderland L2164 (seen here) was set on fire. Personnel boarded the aircraft and temporarily brought the blaze under control. When flames again took hold, L2164 was towed into Mistra Bay and abandoned, eventually settling in the shallows just offshore.

Hurricane V7430 after crashing at Pwales Valley on 28 March 1941. The victor was almost certainly Oberleutnant Joachim Müncheberg. The Hurricane pilot, Sergeant Raymond J. Goode, had recently arrived from the Western Desert on detachment from 274 Squadron. He was hospitalised with shrapnel wounds, but would lose his life just over a year later, on 29 June 1942.

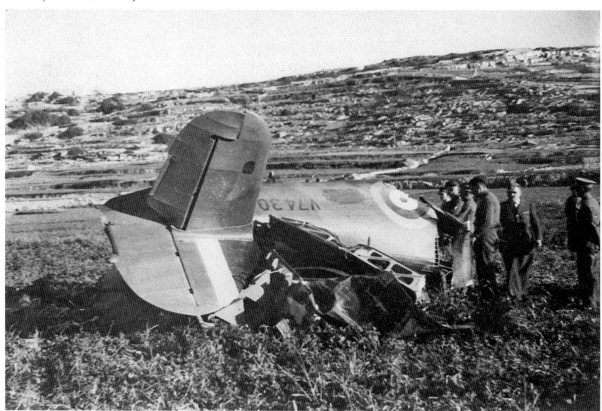

Oberleutnant Joachim Müncheberg is greeted by a celebratory gathering on 28 March 1941 on completion of his 200th combat mission. Müncheberg failed to return from a mission over North Africa on 23 March 1943. His final tally was 135 aircraft destroyed.

During the night of 11/12 April a Ju 87 of *9./St.G.1* was shot down and crashed on to a farmhouse near Għargħur, killing a little girl, Rosaria Mifsud, and seriously injuring another. The pilot, Leutnant Werner Zühlke and wireless operator, Obergefreiter Hans Feldeisen, did not survive. This appears to be the scene soon afterwards.

(**Above and following**) In the morning of Sunday, 27 April 1941 twenty-three Hurricanes took off from the carrier *Ark Royal*. Three FAA Fulmars led the way towards Malta, some 575 miles to the east. En route they were met by a 228 Squadron Sunderland and three Marylands of 69 Squadron, the crews of which were tasked with escorting the new arrivals on the final leg of their journey. Eight Hurricanes and a Fulmar rendezvoused with the Sunderland half an hour behind schedule. They were guided to Malta, arriving while an air raid was in progress. The Sunderland captain, Pilot Officer Leonard G.M. Rees, decided to land as quickly as possible so that the flying-boat might be brought ashore and placed in a hangar, where it would at least be concealed from aerial view. After alighting in Marsaxlokk Bay, Sunderland L5807 was moored at Kalafrana seaplane base. There was just time to adjust one of the beaching legs before the arrival of enemy aircraft compelled the crew and maintenance party to abandon their task. At least two Bf 109s of 7./J.G.26 dived from out of the sun and sped eastwards towards Kalafrana. The flying-boat was shot up, a fuel tank in the starboard wing was punctured and a fire started. Before long the Sunderland was ablaze. It listed to port and sank. Oberleutnant Joachim Müncheberg was duly credited with its destruction. Among the Sunderland's crew was Flying Officer Frank M. Goyen from Australia. In August 1942 he was a flight lieutenant and captain of another Sunderland when it crashed in northern Scotland. There was one survivor. Among the dead was Goyen and a VIP passenger, Prince George, Duke of Kent.

Fighter pilots were, of course, crucial to the survival of Malta. But just as important were those airmen who risked their lives in flying-boats, bombers, torpedo and reconnaissance aircraft, all of which were kept operational through the skills and dedication of often-overworked maintenance crews. Flying Officer Adrian Warburton, seen here with a Martin Maryland, specialised in reconnaissance and was active from the early days of the battle. Warburton was a highly decorated wing commander when he was killed during a sortie over Bavaria on 12 April 1944.

(**Above**) Five Hurricanes of 261 Squadron were shot down or damaged as a result of operations on 11 April. In turn, the RAF claimed at least one Bf109 and a Bf110 destroyed. (The Luftwaffe recorded four losses for *Fliegerkorps X.* on this date.) Pilot Officer Peter Kennett died when he was shot down off the coast and Sergeant Peter H. Waghorn was killed when he crashed on land. Pilot Officers Douglas M. Whitney and Percival A. Mortimer and Sergeant Albert H. Deacon survived after forced/crash-landing their battle-damaged Hurricanes. Three claims for fighters destroyed were submitted by *7.IJ.G.26*: Oberleutnant Joachim Müncheberg was credited with a Hurricane south-east of Malta at 1131 hours and another south-east of St Paul's Bay twenty-two minutes later. Oberleutnant Klaus Mietusch was credited with a Hurricane north of the island at 1150 hours. Italian claims, if any, are unknown. This is Pilot Officer Mortimer's Hurricane V7116. Percival Mortimer died as a result of a flying accident in November 1942.

(**Opposite**) Flying Officer Ernest M. Mason was shot down on 13 April 1941. He was soon rescued by High Speed Launch 107: 'I was shivering with cold so after drying and warming me on shore and temporarily tying string round the artery and dressing the hand I went in an ambulance to hospital. On the way I made the driver stop at the mess and went in for a drink and had a photograph taken in borrowed pyjamas and blue flannel dressing gown.' 'Imshi' Mason was shot down and killed over North Africa on 15 February 1942.

(**Opposite, above**) (*Left to right*) Unteroffizier Paul Kietzmann and Feldwebel Helmut Hartlich, Rudolf Lenzner and Wilhelm Heller of *9./L.G.1* four days before their Ju 88 was shot down over Malta. On 29 April 1941 all were taken prisoner after baling out of their bomber, which had been targeted by AA gunners and Pilot Officers Joseph E. Hall and Anthony J. Rippon (both of 261 Squadron). The German machine crashed at Għajn Tuffieħa (**opposite, below**). Hall survived the war. Anthony Rippon (**above**) died on 25 August 1944.

(**Below**) Undated photograph of 261 Squadron Hurricanes at Ta' Qali.

(**Above**) In April 1941 twenty fighter pilots of C Flight, 261 Squadron, joined ground personnel at Hal Far aerodrome under the command of Squadron Leader Peter W.O. Mould († 1 October 1941). By 7 May C Flight had been reduced to just two serviceable Hurricanes. It remained operational, however, and on 12 May was retitled 185 Squadron. These pilots were among the first to serve in the new unit. (*Back row, left to right*) Flight Lieutenant Charles G. St D. Jeffries, Sergeant Cyril S. Bamberger, Pilot Officer Peter D. Thompson, Pilot Officer Hugh W. 'Chubby' Eliot († 4 March 1945) and Sergeant Basil T. Vardy († 25 September 1943); (*front row, left to right*) Sergeant Arnold W. Jolly, Sergeant Claude G. Hodson, and Sergeant Frank G. Sheppard.

(**Opposite, above**) J. 'Blondie' Johnson, an RAF engine fitter, seen here in mid-1941 with a Mk I Hurricane equipped with overload fuel tanks. This aircraft was probably transiting through Malta en route to the Middle East. It was struck off charge on 2 January 1942 due to battle damage.

(**Opposite, below**) On 21 May 1941 Hurricanes of 249 Squadron arrived at Malta, supposedly in transit to the Middle East. Instead, the pilots were retained and their Hurricanes taken over and flown to Egypt by departing pilots of 261 Squadron (which was then disbanded). Four days later Bf 109s of 7./J.G.26 swept across Ta' Qali aerodrome and shot up 249 Squadron's Hurricanes on the ground as their pilots waited to be scrambled. Flying Officers Eric J.F. Harrington and Patrick H.V. Wells (who was wounded) were able to get out of their aircraft, which were burnt out and destroyed. During the Battle of Britain 249 Squadron had gained a fine reputation and its pilots had perhaps viewed their new posting with some disdain. This attitude did not last.

Sergeant Horace 'Stanley' Burton served in 261 and 185 Squadrons. He would survive the war.

Hawker Hurricane Z2421 after Sergeant Burton accidentally flew into a wrecked hangar at Ħal Far on 11 June 1941.

June (cont.)

The next three weeks - waiting for reinforcements. can be summarised as routine night flying patrols against the odd Italian bomber.

Coming over in small numbers at about 18000 ft they caused great distress to the fish round the Gem of the Med. - tho' they have hit the island once or twice and helped the farmers to scatter the good seed over the land.

It has now been proved conclusively that the I.F.F. does explode when a Hurricane is forced into a langar. Sgt. Burton spent a fortnight in Mtarfa thinking out the results of this expensive experiment and the C.O does not wish for any repetition as results were quite unsuccessful.

Most nights Gremlins were active on the flare path, not only setting fire to P/O Gray's A/c (he was not smoking in the cock-pit at that time), but also attacking with vans and backs of lorries the tail units of the C.O's and F/Lt Jeffries planes.

Other incidents - obviously emanating from tampering with the powers of Darkness - such as Sgt Algernon (I've been here six months) Hodson's preference for landing at Luca and P/O Gray making an approach on the Sunderland flare path in the Bay have filled in the time

Co-incident with the rise of the moon other squadrons braved the night air and dispersed at Safi. They will shortly take their share in night flying and it is hoped that 185 will meet their quota of Macchis on returning to day operations.

Sgt Jolly destroyed a Macchi 200; P/O Barley and Sgt Sheppard shared in the destruction of others. These three have returned to us after temporary loan to 46 & 249 Sqdns.

June 27th & 30th.

About 30 planes (some with hat racks sticking out in front) landed on the Gem of the Med.

Since the diary only respects the truth it must be written that the landings at Hal Far were bloody. Gremlins pushed up and pulled down the surface of the drone as the pilots 'held off' and maintenance crews were seen dashing their heads against brick walls. Technical reasons were given and accepted for the landings made

Sergeant Burton's accident as described in the 'line book' of 185 Squadron.

(**Above**) In July 1941 the Italian Navy's *La Decima Flottiglia MAS* conducted an operation against the British submarine base at Marsamxett Harbour and the newly arrived 'Substance' convoy in neighbouring Grand Harbour. During the night of 25/26 July, two *SLC* 'human torpedoes' and nine *MTM* explosive motorboats were deployed north of the harbour area. The Italians were soon detected. When the attack began, the *SLCs* failed to reach their objectives, which included the destruction of an anti-torpedo net across the harbour entrance. That task was taken over by one of the *MTM* operators. At 0445 hours his *MTM* hit and blew up the mole bridge of the breakwater, causing one span to collapse, effectively blocking the entrance. The attack then turned into a rout for the Italians. Searchlights illuminated the scene and shore defences opened up. At dawn Hurricanes took off to attack survivors as they tried to withdraw. In all, fifteen Italians were killed and eighteen captured. The breakwater bridge remained in disrepair until the construction of a new pedestrian bridge, which was opened in 2012.

(**Opposite, above**) After the Italian raid on Grand Harbour, *MAS 452* was 'captured' by Pilot Officer Denis Winton of 185 Squadron. During an aerial engagement his Hurricane was shot down and Winton baled out into the sea not far from the stationary vessel. He clambered on board, finding only dead Italians, and awaited rescue. This is the recovered torpedo boat at Fort St Angelo.

(**Opposite, below**) Fighter pilots of 185 Squadron on 15 August 1941. (*Back row, left to right*) Pilot Officer Philip M. Allardice († 22 March 1942), Sergeants Arnold Jolly, T.E.J. Ream, C.S. Hunton, Johnny Alderson, A.J. (Jimmy) Forth († 29 December 1941), Ernest G. Knight († 25 October 1941), Brian Hayes († 21 December 1941) and Horsey. (*Middle row*) Pilot Officer R.M. Oliver, Sergeant Trevor H. Bates, Pilot Officer G.G. 'Gay' Bailey († 9 November 1941), Sergeants R.A. (Dicky) Cousens († 21 November 1941), Peter Lillywhite and J.R. Sutherland, Pilot Officer A.J. (Tony) Reeves, Sergeants W.F. Nurse and Basil T. Vardy († 25 September 1943). (*Front row*) Flight Lieutenants S.A.D. Pike and Charles G. St. D. Jeffries, Squadron Leader P.W.O. 'Boy' Mould († 1 October 1941), Flight Lieutenant N.P.W. (Pat) Hancock and Pilot Officer Peter D. Thompson.

Sergeant Arnold Jolly, one of the original members of the newly formed 185 Squadron.

The caption on the back of this photograph reads, 'Crash during dawn landing Aug. 41. No injuries. Sgt/P. Ormiston [and] P/O Blackburn. 126 Sqn.' The Operations Record Book of 126 Squadron is sadly lacking and makes no mention of such an occurrence. That for RAF Station Ta Kali does mention such a crash, but this is stated to have occurred in the morning of 2 July 1941: 'Two Hurricanes collided on landing. Both badly damaged.' Of the two fighter pilots involved, Pilot Officer Charles A. Blackburn did not survive the war, losing his life just over a year later in November 1942.

Pilot Officer Howard M. Coffin (*right*), from California, served in 126 Squadron. *Malta Story*, published in 1943, is very loosely based on Coffin's wartime experiences on the island. Coffin was one of the first Americans to arrive at Malta, together with Pilot Officers Edward E. Steele (posted missing on 19 December 1941), Donald A. Tedford (posted missing on 24 February 1942) and Edward E. Streets. 'Junior' Streets was among six air force personnel who lost their lives when the officers' quarters at Mdina were bombed on 21 March 1942. Only Coffin survived his tour on Malta.

Chapter Four

The Air War: 1942

In November 1941 Generalfeldmarschall Albert Kesselring, commanding *Luftflotte 2* in Russia, was designated Commander-in-Chief South. With the onset of winter, the Germans began to transfer aircraft from Russia and northern Europe south to Sicily. Deteriorating weather conditions might affect flying on the Eastern Front, but air operations could continue elsewhere. On 2 December Adolf Hitler issued Directive No. 38 with the intention of dealing with the ongoing situation in the central Mediterranean, including North Africa and, especially, the problem of Malta. Accordingly, Generalleutnant Bruno Loerzer's *II. Fliegerkorps* took over from the Regia Aeronautica during daylight operations over the island. German raids began on a relatively small scale, increasing in intensity towards the end of the month, with daylight bomber sorties heavily escorted by Bf 109 Fs. On 22 December German units flew for the first time more than 200 sorties against Malta.

(**Opposite, above**) Ju 88 pilots Oberleutnant Viktor Schnez (*left*) and Oberleutnant Georg Lust, photographed in November 1941 south-west of Leningrad on the Eastern Front. Lust was reported missing with his crew during a sortie near Malta on 30 December 1941. Schnez and his crew survived after being shot down on 3 January 1942.

(**Opposite, below**) In September 2000 Viktor Schnez revisited Malta under very different circumstances. Here, he discusses events of 3 January 1942 with eyewitnesses Peter Micallef (*left*) and John Galea (*right*).

The remains of Ju 88 1346/M7+AK of *2./Kampfgruppe 806*. Viktor Schnez recalled his brief period operating over Malta: 'In December 1941 my unit relocated from Germany to Catania. My Staffel was not yet complete when I flew the first missions in the Mediterranean at the end of December. It started on 23.12.41 with a reconnaissance flight over the sea between Malta and the North African coast. After the [Christmas] break, maritime targets in this area were to be bombed on 30.12.41 as part of an "armed reconnaissance" (with bombs on board). As no ships were sighted at that time, I jettisoned the bombs diving over Valletta harbour. The third mission was a dive attack on Luqa airfield on 03.01.42. We approached at an altitude of 4,000 metres, dived and released the bombs at an altitude of 1,000 metres. After the machine levelled out at about 600 metres I climbed and set course for Sicily. I had to fly over the island in a northerly direction, when we were engaged by anti-aircraft defences and several Hurricanes simultaneously. First, the latter hit the cooling system of the left engine, thus putting it out of service. By now I had cleared the coast at an altitude of 2,000 metres and was already flying over the sea when, following renewed attacks, the right engine caught fire. In order not to ditch in the water yet again – previously I had already become well acquainted with conditions at sea after a belly-landing in the northern Baltic and a subsequent 85-hour trip in a rubber dinghy – I headed back to Malta, intending to bale out of the aircraft over the island. The English anti-aircraft defences, which had fired at us during the attack and as we took off, decently ceased firing when our burning machine returned. I twice gave the order: "*aussteigen! aussteigen!*" ["Get out! Get out!"] My crew could jump "at their leisure" while I held the aircraft on a straight course. Only after I had left the controls did the machine go into a high-speed vertical descent. When I tried to get out, I realised that I had not disconnected the [headphones] wireless cable. It took time to pull out the plug, so I only managed to exit the machine at the last moment. After the third attempt, I managed to pull a handle [ripcord] on the parachute belt in free fall and thus deploy the parachute. Very soon afterwards I landed next to the debris of my blown-up aircraft. Due to a bullet wound in my upper left arm, I was transferred to a field hospital after a short interrogation. There I learned from the local press that I had supposedly carried out a "kamikaze attack", presumably because I had left the aircraft so late close to the airfield. But for me it was anything but a kamikaze death.'

Hurricanes of 185 Squadron at Hal Far start up and taxi out during a scramble.

(**Above**) In the afternoon of 9 March 1942 twelve Ju 88s and eleven Bf 109s, some armed with bombs, targeted Ħal Far, Luqa and Safi. Although there was no aerial opposition, the raiders faced both light and heavy AA fire and a Ju 88 of 6./K.G.77 was shot down at Ħal Far. The pilot, Oberleutnant Gerhard Becker, and rear gunner, Unteroffizier Anton Schweiger, were killed. The observer, Unteroffizier Arnulf Thiemann, died later in hospital. Only the wireless operator, Unteroffizier Walter Kunzi, survived. In this dramatic image, a parachute can just be seen descending over the burning wreck of the Ju 88.

(**Opposite, above**) Ħal Far was home to 185 Squadron – Malta's longest-serving wartime fighter unit – but also served as a base for FAA aircraft, such as this Albacore.

(**Opposite, below**) According to the original caption in the photograph album of Ernie Broad (185 Squadron), this Albacore 'crashed on landing after being shot up whilst in action – The crew were killed.'

FAA aircrew at Ħal Far, probably in 1942.

Detail from a photograph of a Messerschmitt Bf 109 during a low-level strafe of Ħal Far aerodrome. This method of attack was a risky business for German fighter pilots. In February and April 1942 three Bf 109 pilots were killed when they were shot down close to Ħal Far.

According to the image caption, these German fighter pilots have just returned from a mission to Malta in late March 1942. The central figure is almost certainly Major Herbert Kaminski, *Gruppenkommandeur* of *I./J.G.53*. Kaminski survived the war.

(**Opposite and above**) On 14 April 1942 Hauptmann Karl-Heinz Krahl, *Kommandeur* of *Stab II./J.G.3*, was shot down by ground fire during a low-level strafe, crashing near Ħal Far. The *Balkenkreuz* from a wing of Krahl's Bf 109 became a feature in photographs of 185 Squadron personnel. This is Flight Lieutenant Rhys M. Lloyd (reported missing near El Alamein on 27 October 1942).

On 8 May 1942 Unteroffizier Heinrich Becker of *8./J.G.53* was shot down for the second time in less than a fortnight. Previously he had been rescued after baling out and landing in the sea but this time Becker was taken prisoner. His Bf 109 crashed at Marsa Sports Club, providing an ideal photo opportunity for the local press.

H.M. KING GEORGE VI
AWARDED TO MALTA
The "GEORGE CROSS"
ON THE 956th DAY
OF THE WAR
APRIL 15th 1942

TIMES OF MALTA

No. 2,094   PRICE 2d.   **MONDAY, MAY 11, 1942**

BATTLE OF MALTA : AXIS HEAVY LOSSES

'SPITFIRES' SLAUGHTER 'STUKAS'

BRILLIANT TEAM WORK OF A.A. GUNNERS AND R.A.F.

63 Enemy Aircraft Destroyed Or Damaged Over Malta Yesterday

THE total number of enemy losses over Malta today (Sunday) is:—

Destroyed 22 — probably destroyed 20 — damaged 21

The specification of these is as follows:—

	DESTROYED	Probably Destroyed	Damaged
R.A.F. —	12 bombers	11 bombers	11 bombers
	4 fighters	9 fighters	10 fighters

ANTI-AIRCRAFT ARTILLERY —
5 bombers   (Several more enemy aircraft were damaged by
1 fighter   Anti-Aircraft Artillery that were probably later
destroyed by our fighters).

The last two days have seen a metamorphosis in the Battle of Malta. After two days of the fiercest aerial combat that has ever taken place over the Island the Luftwaffe, with its Italian lackeys, has taken the most formidable beating that has been known since the Battle of Britain two and a half years ago. Indeed, in proportion to the numbers of aircraft involved, this trouncing is even greater than the Germans suffered at that time.

It has always been known that man for man, and machine for machine, the R.A.F. were infinitely superior to the Hun, and everybody looked forward to the day when he could be met on terms of parity, for they looked upon the outcome as a certainty. That day has arrived — the R.A.F. even has numerical superiority over its fighter opponents for the first time — and the results have excelled the most optimistic expectations. Our fighters have formed, with the A.A. Artillery, a team which has dealt out appalling destruction on the enemy.

COURAGE OF MALTA'S GUNNERS

Teamwork has been the watchword during all these weary months of taking a pounding, with very little else to do than grin and bear it. And if during the last couple of days the R.A.F. have been more in the limelight than the gunners, over the whole period of Malta's affliction they must be looked upon as a brilliant forward line, supported by equally magnificent backs, who have never once let anyone down. For months on end these gunners have hurled steel and defiance at the enemy, no matter what the circumstances. They have been subjected to probably the most diabolical bombing that gunners have ever known, they have been ceaselessly machine-gunned; they have suffered casualties, but others have taken their places in nobly as those who died; if we're badly wounded. Yet never once have they faltered, and their total of 101 enemy aircraft destroyed in April alone was a fitting climax to 5 months of magnificent steady achievement. Above all, their courage, at times under most distressing conditions, has been superb. The people of Malta owe them a debt which is incalculable.

APRIL ORDEAL

Since the beginning of April this Island has endured the saddest phase in her career — until yesterday. She has been pounded without ceasing, and certain damage have prevented much in the way of getting back on the scale which was desired. But yesterday it was known that the boot was on the other foot. The Hun realised it, too, at the last moment. He set about the problem as he thought, with the same insolent ease as that to which he has hitherto thought he was entitled. He set out to immolate our aircraft on their aerodromes in the same methodical positions way which he has always used. Little and often seemed to be his policy, and there were five raids during the day. Mr. Feinberg, and the Italians, who are him from a prodigious height, came to as usual with their fighter escort in swarms.

SHATTERING SHOCK FOR THE HUN

But he got a shattering shock. Instead of finding on the ground our fighters were in the air, waiting to meet them. They chased the fighters and attacked some bombers before they rained quite a flew
(Continued on Page 4, Col. 5)

what it was all about. For the first time for a great while the R.A.F. met the enemy on equal or better terms, and at the end of the day he retired to lick gaping wounds which he had never anticipated. Thirty of his aircraft, with the help of the gunners, had been badly mauled, and of these 7 had been shot down out of the sky, and a further 7 had little hope of getting home.

SALUTARY LESSON FOR ITALIANS

During the afternoon's raids the sky looked like the outside of some fantastic wasps' nest, with aircraft milling about in a breathless, hectic rough-house. The noise of cannon and machine-gun was all the sweeter for the fact that half at least of them were for once on our side. That being so, nobody on the ground had the slightest qualms about the result. Nor did the R.A.F. fail to take full advantage of the position. They chased their opposite numbers all round the sky, and hurled themselves at the bombers. The Ital ans especially got a military lesson which it is hoped that they will not forget for their own sakes. Their usual five bombers were seen crossing the sky in their usual tight vic formation, not varying their height, and as though their pilots had their eyes glued to a spot on an extremely high horizon. But what was not usual was the fact that of its five only two limped back to base. Spitfires had sent the other three hurtling into what they claim to be the sea and two of the other fighters most probably followed them.

Today (Sunday) the good work has been carried on even more successfully. This morning German bombers came over to try to cause more havoc in the already stricken dock and area. Again they met a task which surprised them, for they were convinced — why a pall of smoke and the prospect of a grim game of blind man's buff where they touched the various R.A.F. fighters died before some of them into dropping their bombs into the sea. Those that survived found fighters waiting for them, as they pulled out of their dive and for some minutes there was mad pandemonium, with bombs, heavy and light A.A., ammunition and machine-guns forming a british cacophony of sound. Most of them made the attack under cover...

MUSSOLINI'S MISCALCULATION

Mr Churchill delivered his broadcast on the second anniversary of... entrusted with the offi... in He spoke of the ... in this World War.
(Continued at foot of...)

EASTERN FRONT

Strong Russian Attacks
(Reuter's Service)

LONDON, May 10

Strong Russian attacks supported by tanks and artillery on the northern front in the Lake Ilmen region in one where the Russian tanks broke through the German lines, are reported by a High Command survey given over the German radio.

The break-through occurred south-east of Lake Ilmen when several Russian infantry regiments supported by 46 tanks launched an assault on a four-mile front held by a German infantry division. The report admits that "individual" tanks broke through.

Fighting on the Kalinin Front is reported in a supplement to Sunday's Soviet communique. Here, in two days, the Germans lost 600 Officers and Men in killed alone. Artillery operating on the Russian guards on the Smolensk front destroyed 5 German blockhouses and German artillery.

The supplement adds that a German prisoner states that the first German Tank Division lost one half of its effectives in recent fighting on the Eastern Front.

CHURCHILL'S STIRRING BROADCAST

A Tribute To Malta
(Reuter's Service)   LONDON, May 10

In the course of his world-wide broadcast tonight (Sunday) the Prime Minister Mr. Churchill, paid a tribute to Malta and welcomed back General Dobbie, for nearly two years, "the heroic defender of Malta." For the moment it looks as if the terrific air attack on Malta had slackened.

"It looks," said the Prime Minister, as if a lot of enemy aircraft have been moved eastwards. If so, this supreme air battle for Malta, upon which they have concentrated such an immense preponderance of strength and for which they sacrificed so many aircraft, will have been definitely won.

GENERAL DOBBIE AND LORD GORT

Paying a tribute to the leadership of General Dobbie, Mr. Churchill said that after two years of battle the Governor of Malta was taking a well-earned repose.

Of the new Governor, the Prime Minister said that he knew of no man in the British Empire to whom he would sooner entrust the combating and beating down of other perils that may beset Malta.

A STERN WARNING

Germany was warned by Mr. Church ll that if Hitler used poison gas against Russia, Britain would use her growing air superiority to carry the warfare on the largest possible scale against military objectives in Germany.

"Such use of poison gas against France by Germany would be treated as if it were used against the British Isles and at a time for Hitler to choose whether he wished to add that additional horror to aerial warfare."

BOMBING OFFENSIVE

The British and American bombing offensive against Germany would be one of the principal features of this year's world war. Now was the time to use Britain's increasingly superior air strength to strike hard and continually at the German home front, which remained the foundation of the whole enormous German invasion of Russia.

FAR EAST

Chinese Successes

CHUNGKING, May 10

THE Japanese retreating in the south-west of Yunnan are suffering heavy casualties with the Chinese tightening the ring round them, says the communique.

There is nothing to suggest the truth of the Axis reports that British forces in the Chindwin valley are about to be exterminated it was stated authoritatively in London on Sunday. The latest information is that the British force is withdrawing up the valley in good order.

MIDDLE EAST FRONT
(Reuter's Service)

CAIRO, May 10

The Middle East communique today (Sunday) says: "Some small enemy columns including tanks and artillery withdrew on being engaged by our light forces."

Nothing was known in London on Sunday of the claim that the Axis powers landed airborne troops in the Marmarica desert which forms the eastern end of Cyrenaica, and destroyed petrol and oil dumps.

Twenty-two were killed and forty wounded in an air raid at Alexandria early on Sunday morning, says a Ministry of the Interior communique.

MALTA PROGRAMME FROM AMERICA TODAY

There will be a Special "March of Time" Programme from the United States about Malta on the African Service of the B.B.C. from 5.30 to 6.30 p.m. (local time) today, Monday, May 11, 1942.

STOP PRESS

WASHINGTON, May 11.—The attack on Tokyo on April 18 was made by America's Army bombers. From low altitude, military, naval and industrial plants were bombed in the vicinity of Tokyo, unmistakably and accurately. Large fires were started which in some instances burned for two days.—Reuter

CHUNGKING, May 10.—Attempting to break through the Chinese cordon by a thrust across the Yunnan border in the Chefang area, the Japanese have lost 3,000 men killed, according to tonight's Chinese communique.—Reuter.

MOSCOW, May 10.—Yesterday, says the Soviet midnight communique, 29 Nazi aircraft were destroyed on the Russian Front. The Red Air Force lost 15 planes.—(Reuter).

Mussolini had miscalculated the strength of Britain and the Empire, and how Italy's African Empire had been liquidated.

(We shall be publishing the text of Mr. Churchill's stirring broadcast in Tuesday's Times of Malta.)

ANGORA, May 10.—A Reuter bulletin...

(**Opposite**) Australian Sergeant J.L. 'Tony' Boyd (185 Squadron) was scrambled twice on 14 May. At 1248 hours his Spitfire was downed by an unidentified fighter and crashed on the north-western perimeter of Luqa aerodrome. Tony Boyd, due to stand down prior to his imminent return to the United Kingdom, did not survive.

(**Above**) Soon after Sergeant Boyd's demise, a Ju 88 of *1./K.Gr.806* crashed on the northern perimeter of Ta' Qali aerodrome. Among those involved in shooting down the bomber in conjunction with AA gunners were Flight Lieutenant Denis A. Barnham and New Zealander Pilot Officer M.R.B. (Bruce) Ingram of 601 Squadron and Flying Officer Richard Mitchell and Flight Sergeant John Hurst of 603 Squadron. The latter's squadron leader, Lord David Douglas-Hamilton, was one of many eye-witnesses, recalling: 'The 88 jettisoned its bombs at the edge of the aerodrome, then did a drunken swoop across the aerodrome, and one of its engines fell out. It crashed just beside the landing ground and burned furiously with columns of black smoke. We got out of our slit trench and cheered. I went round to look at the wreckage. It was well smashed up. The pilot was reclining backwards in the front of the wreckage, quite dead, but still grasping the control column. He had evidently been trying to control the aeroplane until the end. Soon there was little left of him or the 88.' A series of photographs was taken of the unfortunate crewman trapped among the burning wreckage. These images were especially sought-after among Malta-based personnel.

Flight Lieutenant Denis Barnham in Spitfire 'U', the same aircraft he flew on 14 May 1942 when he was involved in bringing down the Ju 88 that crashed at Ta' Qali. After the war Barnham wrote *One Man's Window*, a book based on his wartime Malta diary.

A photograph album that belonged to Denis Barnham includes this picture of Australian Pilot Officer Thomas W. Scott, Barnham, Australian Pilot Officer G.M. (Max) Briggs († 10 May 1942) and Pilot Officer Bruce Ingram († 11 July 1944).

In his book *One Man's Window*, Denis Barnham makes reference to a hilltop vantage point at Naxxar, from where observers could watch dogfights overhead. This would appear to be the place.

This Re.2001 crash-landed alongside Fort San Leonardo after an encounter with Spitfires on 18 May. The pilot, Tenente Remo Cazzolli of *152ª Squadriglia C.T.*, was badly injured but survived.

Among those who may have attacked Tenente Cazzolli's Reggiane was Australian Sergeant V.P. (Paul) Brennan. He is seen here (*left*) with his close friend in 249 Squadron R.B. (Ray) B. Hesselyn of New Zealand. Brennan and Hesselyn subsequently co-authored the book *Spitfires over Malta* in collaboration with journalist C.H. (Henry) Bateson. Paul Brennan died as a result of a flying accident on 13 June 1943.

(**Above**) Three pilot officers enjoy a day off at the Dragunara Palace, St Julians. On the left is Donald E. Llewellyn, soon to join 601 Squadron in the Middle East. To his left are Canadians A.A. (Andy) McNaughton and J.F. (Jimmy) Lambert of 185 Squadron. Neither Lambert nor McNaughton survived the war. McNaughton was shot down and killed on 1 June, not long after this photo was taken. Lambert took over 421 (Royal Canadian Air Force) Squadron on 13 December 1943. He was reported missing over northern France one week later, during his first operational flight as squadron leader.

(**Opposite, above**) SNCOs John W. Yarra (Australia) and, on his left, C.E. (Ernie) Broad (UK) with Spitfire BR294/GL-E, which they each flew until it was written off in a landing accident on 2 July 1942. Both pilots would finish their tours on Malta. 'Slim' Yarra was killed not long afterwards, on 10 December 1942.

(**Opposite, below**) Flight Lieutenant Ronald West, seen here with his ground crew in mid-1942, was an experienced fighter pilot who joined 185 Squadron as a flight commander from 249 Squadron. On 23 May 1944 Ronnie West, then in 610 Squadron, crashed on landing and suffered serious burns. He later died of his injuries.

(**Above**) 'Erks', or ground crew, kept Malta's aircraft operational. These men of 185 Squadron pose near Ħal Far's operations shelter. (**Below**) Crew of Spitfire 'B' (185 Squadron).

Crew with Spitfire BR294 'E' (185 Squadron).

Squadron Leader Lord David Douglas-Hamilton (centre) with fellow fighter pilots of 603 Squadron in mid-1942.

(**Above**) Early on 4 July ten Spitfires of 249 Squadron were scrambled to intercept three Savoia-Marchetti S.84s that arrived with a large number of fighters. At least two bombers were shot down. One, a *14ª Squadriglia B.T.* machine, fell between Għaxaq and Birżebbuġa. The wireless operator, Aviere Scelto Arduino Pelleschi, who was severely wounded, baled out and was taken prisoner. He was the only survivor.

(**Opposite, above**) Canadian Sergeant Daniel J. Hartney was injured in this landing accident on 19 July, soon after joining 185 Squadron. Hartney later fell ill and died in January 1943 while en route to the UK.

(**Opposite, below**) Malta's most successful fighter pilot was another Canadian, Sergeant George F. 'Screwball' Beurling of 249 Squadron. On 27 July he shot down Sergente Maggiore Faliero Gelli of *378ª Squadriglia C.T.*, who crash-landed this Macchi C.202 at Gozo and was taken prisoner.

George Beurling with the rudder and 'cat and mice' squadron emblem from Faliero Gelli's Macchi. In 1943 Beurling collaborated with Leslie Roberts to produce the book, *Malta Spitfire*. He would lose his life in an aircraft crash in Italy on 20 May 1948.

Chapter Five

Artillery and the PBI

Sometimes, attacking Axis aircraft encountered no aerial opposition and on those occasions especially, Malta was reliant on its anti-aircraft gunners. For a small island, Malta fielded a formidable number of 4.5-inch, 3.7-inch (static and mobile) and 3-inch (semi-mobile) HAA guns.

(**Opposite, above**) As the war continued, reinforcements were shipped to the beleaguered island. On 10 January 1941 personnel of 190th HAA Battery (originally part of 69th HAA Regiment Royal Artillery) reached Malta. By August 1943 there were 111 HAA guns situated throughout the island.

(**Opposite, below**) In July 1941 Operation 'Substance' delivered to Malta supplies and personnel, including gunners of 4th HAA Regiment RA. On 23 July the British cruiser *Manchester* and the destroyer *Fearless* were severely damaged during an Italian aerial attack. *Manchester* was able to withdraw to Gibraltar, but *Fearless* had to be sunk to avoid capture. HMS *Fearless* is seen ablaze in this photo taken from the merchantman *Port Chalmers*.

(**Opposite, above**) On 27 July 1941 'Substance' reached Malta. Personnel, including artillerymen, disembark at Grand Harbour from the Australian destroyer *Nestor*.

(**Opposite, below**) Malta was also defended by 40mm Bofors LAA guns, such as this one in a dangerously exposed position overlooking Grand Harbour in 1942. The helmets worn by these gunners are painted in the distinctive 'rubble wall' camouflage scheme that was unique to Malta-based personnel.

(**Above**) By August 1943 there were 182 Bofors guns on Malta. These could be static, mobile or semi-mobile. These Bofors of an unidentified LAA unit are at the nineteenth-century Fort Spinola – since demolished and today the site of the Portomaso redevelopment.

(**Above**) Bofors of the same unidentified LAA unit, this time in the area of St Paul's Bay.

(**Opposite, above**) A Bofors crew during a quiet period at their gun position at Ta' Xbiex, overlooking Marsamxett Harbour and the submarine base at Manoel Island.

(**Opposite, below**) Ground forces also occupied defences and beach posts and manned machine-gun positions, such as these Lewis guns at XHB 8, a gun site of 5 Battery, 4th HAA Regiment, located at Il-Mara (Benghisa), part of the base defences of Ħal Far, Safi and Kalafrana.

(**Above**) A 3.7-inch gun at XHB 8.

(**Opposite, above**) Timed exposure photograph of a night raid, showing tracer fire and searchlights over Malta. Searchlights were essential for illuminating targets.

(**Opposite, below**) 20 July 1942. S.F. (Stan) Fraser of 4th HAA Regiment took this photograph of a Ju 88 of 8./K.G.77 as it crashed at Kirkop (*flash right of centre*). All the crew died. Another raider (*top left*) is illuminated by searchlight. HAA guns – probably XHE 24M at Il-Marnisi – can also be seen firing (*far right*). Afterwards, Stan wrote in his diary: 'I could see the target, already illuminated at the apex of a concentration of searchlight beams. The moon was almost full &, with the searchlights, caused a beautiful pool of light to be reflected in the waters of the bay below. I ran for my camera, & placed it in a good position to take a time exposure by the aid of this light and also by the lights of the guns which intermittently flashed, as the enemy planes were greeted by the gunners. Within a minute of the plane being caught in the beams, it crashed near the centre of the island and burst into flame. I took a photo just as it crashed.'

Lieutenant Clifford A.L. Clark of the Royal West Kent Regiment with twin-Vickers machine guns at defence post LQ8 at Luqa aerodrome. The role on Malta of the 'poor bloody infantry' – the PBI – is often ignored or over-looked. In 1942 there were on the island eleven British infantry battalions, together with four battalions of The King's Own Malta Regiment. 2nd Battalion The Devonshire Regiment, 1st Battalion The Hampshire Regiment and 1st Battalion The Dorsetshire Regiment later fought in Sicily and Italy as 231 Infantry Brigade before being withdrawn to take part in the Normandy landings. 4th Battalion The Royal East Kent Regiment (The Buffs) was deployed to the Aegean together with 234 Infantry Brigade, comprising 1st Battalion The Durham Light Infantry, 2nd Battalion The Royal Irish Fusiliers (Faughs) and 2nd Battalion The Queen's Own Royal West Kent Regiment, only to be annihilated while defending the islands of Kos and Leros in late 1943. 8th (Ardwick) Battalion The Manchester Regiment went to the Middle East and later Italy. 8th Battalion The King's Own Royal Regiment (Lancaster) also deployed to the Middle East before ending up in Italy and being re-designated 1st Battalion (the original 1st Battalion having wiped out at Leros). 11th Battalion The Lancashire Fusiliers would fight in Italy, while 1st Battalion The Cheshire Regiment ended the war in north-west Europe.

Lieutenant Clifford Clark's combined army and RAF team at LQ8. Clark explained: 'I was the Liaison Officer with the R.A.F. to inform R.A.F. H.Q. by land telephone or if this was damaged by despatch rider of all incidents on the 'drome, which included my having the similar authority of a Wing Commander to scramble fighter squadrons. During this time, I became particularly friendly and concerned with 601 (City of London) Spitfire Squadron. At that stage … my platoon was engaged, amongst other things, in helping to repair the runways, building aircraft pens, and helping the R.A.F. ground teams to service and turn round the aircraft.' Clark is the officer with binoculars; the corporal is George Hatcher. In November 1943 both would evade capture on Leros before escaping to Turkey.

Officers of the Royal Irish Fusiliers at Naxxar, Malta, on St Patrick's Day, 1943, shortly before deploying to the Middle East and, ultimately, Leros.

Chapter Six

Malta Convoys

Malta could not have survived without resupply. The Royal Navy and Allied merchant ships sustained heavy losses in the relentless effort to bring to the island personnel, victuals, military stores and equipment, not least ammunition and aviation fuel.

(**Opposite, above**) At about 0115 hours on 12 February 1942 the destroyer HMS *Maori* was bombed and sunk at No. 3 Buoy at Grand Harbour. The wreck was subsequently removed to nearby Marsamxett Harbour. (The forepart remains in shallow water just west of Fort St Elmo.) In this photo, the partially submerged *Maori* is visible in the light of the flare right of frame.

(**Opposite, below**) On 20 March 1942 convoy 'MW10' departed Egypt for Malta. SS *Clan Campbell* was attacked and sunk en route. While assisting the commissioned auxiliary supply ship *Breconshire*, the destroyer HMS *Southwold* struck a mine and was lost. Following the arrival at Malta of *Breconshire* and the merchantmen *Pampas* and *Talabot* (seen here), the Luftwaffe directed its efforts against the ports. As a result of heavy raids on 26 March, direct hits were made on the three merchant ships. Within days all would be written off. Additional losses included the Royal Fleet Auxiliary *Plumleaf*, the already damaged submarine *P39* and the destroyer HMS *Legion*.

(**Opposite, above**) *Talabot* on fire, probably on 26 March 1942.

(**Opposite, below**) On 10 May 1942 HMS *Gallant* lost her bow when she struck a mine. The destroyer was beached at Grand Harbour, near the wreck of *Talabot*.

(**Above**) As well as carrying out offensive operations, submarines also ferried supplies to Malta. This is Lazzaretto at Manoel Island, which served as a submarine base and as such was a major target during air attacks.

Leichter Kreuzer „Penelope" im Dock von La Valletta.
MALTA.

4.4.42.

M. 1:1.300

Zerstörungen durch Bombentreffer

Einschlag
einer 1000 kg-Bombe

O.B.S. / LcBild / Bildstelle mot.

This Luftwaffe aerial photograph shows the cruiser HMS *Penelope* in No. 4 dock at French Creek (Grand Harbour) on 4 April 1942. During this time the ship would become so holed with bomb splinters that she would earn the nickname 'Pepperpot'. HMS *Penelope* was torpedoed and lost with more than 400 of her crew on 18 February 1944.

THE STARBOARD SIDE OF H.M.S. "PENELOPE" after heavy attack by enemy aircraft in the Mediterranean : There are hundreds of holes, from fragments of the bombs dropped near her whilst in Malta Harbour, and these were all plugged before she sailed for Gibraltar

From *The Sphere*, 27 June 1942.

Malta Dockyard remained in operation throughout the siege. This is French Creek, facing Senglea. According to the caption of this undated press photograph, a 4-inch gun is being replaced on a warship.

(**Opposite, above**) Of all the Malta convoys, Operation 'Pedestal' is undoubtedly the best known. On 3 August 1942 'Pedestal' left Scotland for the Mediterranean. Of fourteen merchant vessels, *Deucalion*, *Empire Hope*, *Clan Ferguson*, *Waimarama*, *Almeria Lykes*, *Wairangi*, *Glenorchy*, *Santa Elisa* and *Dorset* were lost, together with the carrier HMS *Eagle*, the cruisers *Cairo* and *Manchester*, and the destroyer *Foresight*. *Rochester Castle*, *Melbourne Star*, *Port Chalmers*, *Brisbane Star* and *Ohio* reached Malta. This is either HMS *Victorious* or *Indomitable* on 12 August.

(**Opposite, below**) Detail from an aerial photograph taken on 12 August during an attack that left the carrier *Indomitable* (2) severely damaged. Forty-eight were killed or died of their injuries; four pilots were lost and more than fifty all ranks were wounded. Cruiser (1) at centre is probably HMS *Charybdis*.

3 „Hurricane" auf Deck

Flugzeugtr. v. Typ „ILLUSTRIOUS"
M. ~1:1400

O.B.S./Bildst. mot.

Fl. G.B/See 0754 SG/14
v. 12.8.42   13³⁰ Uhr

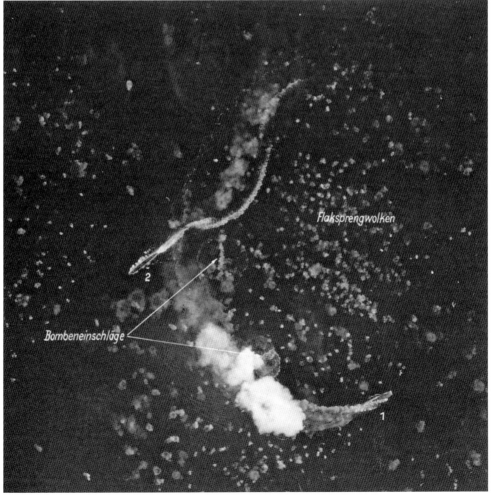

Flaksprengwolken

2

Bombeneinschläge

1

The next morning, 13 August, *Waimarama* was sunk.

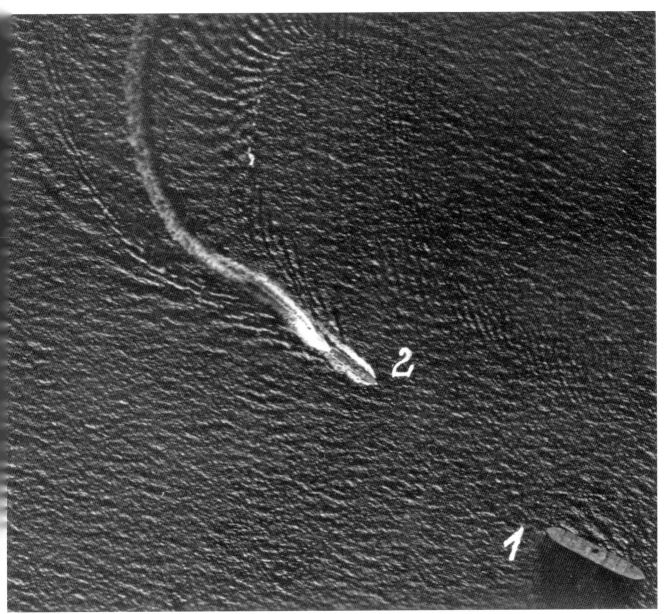

Another Luftwaffe aerial image, this one taken at 1315 hours on 13 August, showing a destroyer approaching a stationary freighter. Of the four surviving merchantmen, the Texaco oil tanker *Ohio* came to symbolise the Malta convoys. After being disabled during torpedo and bombing attacks, during which one bomber crashed onto her deck, the battered ship was guided into Grand Harbour lashed between two destroyers, and with another secured to the stern. The date was 15 August, the Feast of the Assumption, known locally as the Feast of St Mary. Ever since, the Maltese have referred to Operation 'Pedestal' as *Il-Konvoj ta' Santa Marija*. It cost the lives of up to 387 seamen, 28 Fleet Air Arm personnel and 25 personnel of the Maritime Regiment RA. In the air there were also losses on both sides.

A Royal Navy escort vessel enters Grand Harbour, cheered by spectators from vantage points around the port.

Chapter Seven

The Most Bombed Place on Earth

Alan M. Moorehead is credited with the oft-repeated statement that Malta became 'the most bombed place on earth'. In 1940 those on Malta had enough to contend with during ongoing air attacks by the Regia Aeronautica, but those who survived the war invariably agree that Italian raids were far less severe in comparison to what followed when the Luftwaffe joined the fray. The Germans were an altogether different foe from the Italians. They were more determined and often displayed almost reckless courage during attacks.

(**Opposite, above**) This dramatic photograph, included in spite of its poor quality, is indicative of the ferocity of raids carried out by the Luftwaffe. Here, a Ju 87 Stuka dives over Senglea, just 100 metres or so above the rooftops. The likely target is shipping in the adjacent Dockyard Creek.

(**Opposite, below**) Of considerably better quality than the previous image, this photograph appears to have been taken at the end of the raid.

(**Above**) Service personnel clearing up after Upper Barrakka is severely damaged in a bombing raid.

(**Opposite, above**) Bomb craters and damaged hangars at Kalafrana seaplane base, situated on the south-east coast, not far from Ħal Far aerodrome. The area has since been redeveloped as a container terminal, so that nothing remains today of the former RAF station.

(**Opposite, below**) The view from inside a bomb-damaged hangar at Kalafrana.

(**Opposite, above**) The Dockyard area, aerodromes and other military installations were the main targets of both the Regia Aeronautica and the Luftwaffe. These are barrack buildings at Hal Far.

(**Opposite, below**) View from a reinforced military position during what appears to be a raid in progress.

(**Above**) Many bombs failed to detonate. Numerous unexploded bombs (UXBs) were dealt with by bomb disposal personnel.

At Ħal Far aerodrome a simple solution was to push UXBs off a nearby cliff into the sea. Canadian J.M. (Matt) Reid, who served as a fighter pilot in 185 Squadron, recalled that eventually, 'This collection let go with such a wallop that caused a mushroom column of seawater, sand, grit, etc. ... covering the whole area with the slurry substance. I have never heard of it being reported. The evidence was the scar slashed on the sea cliff hundreds of feet high and gouging out a large area.'

This German parachute mine is believed to have dropped near Mdina where it was made safe on 23 May 1941 by Electrical Lieutenant Antony G. Rogers and Commissioned Boatswain L.J. Herbert Sheldon. Both were recipients of the George Medal. They were killed the same day while attending to another device.

Looking north-east along Merchants Street, Valletta. There is no date or caption to indicate with certainty what is happening, but it seems that a bomb may have fallen in the vicinity.

(**Opposite, above**) Inevitably, and at times possibly intentionally, bombs often fell in residential areas.

(**Opposite, below**) Bomb damage along the coast road near St Anne Square, Sliema.

Graffiti expressing the feelings of one man in particular but shared, no doubt, by the majority at the time.

(**Opposite**) A particularly grim day for Malta was 21 March 1942. At 1436 hours there was a heavy raid that continued for more than two hours. Bf 109s escorted up to seventy or more Ju 88s, with Ta' Qali the main target. No Hurricanes were scrambled, but anti-aircraft gunners claimed three Ju 88s destroyed and three others damaged. Initial reports indicated that in four residential areas 135 civilians were killed, seriously injured or buried under debris. In Mosta twenty-four people died and nearly twice as many were injured when the ceiling of a rock shelter collapsed. A bomb that landed next to the Point de Vue hotel at Rabat took the lives of Flight Lieutenant Cecil Baker (126 Squadron), Pilot Officers John Booth (249 Squadron), Australian, James Guerin (249 Squadron), William Hallett (126 Squadron), American, Edward Streets (126 Squadron), Flying Officer (Acting Flight Lieutenant) Arthur Waterfield (Intelligence Officer) and a civilian, Dominic Ceci.

(**Above**) By the time this photograph was taken the worst was over. These children are shown in late 1942 among the ruins of what is almost certainly one of the Three Cities surrounding Grand Harbour.

(**Opposite, above**) Spitfires of 229 Squadron at Krendi (Qrendi) aerodrome, inaugurated as an RAF fighter station in November 1942.

(**Opposite, below**) 185 Squadron baseball team, January–February 1943. (*Standing, left to right*) Pilot Officer Stamford S. 'Bill' Williams from New Zealand († 22 December 1944), Canadians Sergeant W.A. (Al) Laing and Flight Sergeant John N. 'Dusty' Miller († 20 March 1943), American Pilot Officer A.F. (Al) Eckert and, behind, Canadian Flying Officer E.G. (Gordon) Lapp, Englishman Sergeant James Tarbuck († 1 April 1943), Sergeant George F. Mercer from Canada, Squadron Leader John H. Ashton (UK), Flight Lieutenant Harold C. Knight from South Africa († 21 May 1944), Flying Officer Len Cheek (UK) and Canadian Sergeant G.D. 'Jerry' Billing. (*Kneeling*) Canadians Flight Sergeant Cornelius J. Carmody († 8 February 1943), Sergeant J.M. Maffre, Sergeant George C. Warcup, Flight Sergeant R.A.G. (Georges) Nadon, Flight Sergeant D.J. McLaren and from the UK, Sergeant J.D. Thorogood.

Spitfire over Mdina, Malta's ancient former capital, probably in late 1942 or early 1943.

On 11 October the Luftwaffe and the Regia Aeronautica launched the first in a series of attacks on Malta. This, the final Axis offensive, would continue for one week before the Luftwaffe changed its strategy. Daylight bomber sorties were then replaced by fighter sweeps and fighter-bomber attacks. After the siege was lifted, Axis attacks continued, albeit on a much reduced scale and with less frequency. On 5 May 1943 *Ritterkreuzträger* Oberleutnant Günther Hannak, *Staffelkapitän* of 7./J.G.27, became the only German pilot to successfully force land his aircraft at Malta. The Bf 109 G was seized intact. Hannak's interrogator subsequently recorded:

'P/W took off with 9 other a/c of his Staffel from BISCARI at about 1215 hrs. to carry out a recco over MALTA. P/W was the Staffelkapitaen and led the formation. He was flying an a/c belonging to another member of his Staffel as his own a/c was u/s. The G P + I Z had been flown to BISCARI earlier the same morning.

'The formation flew more or less due South and made landfall approximately over COMINO at about 22/24.000 ft. It was at this point that P/W noticed that his cockpit was filling with smoke and oil was splashing on to his windscreen. He estimated his speed at this time at 500 k.p.h.. The a/c continued crossing the island and when over the sea P/W realised it was hopeless to continue. He jettisoned his cockpit cover, which also carried away his oxygen mask, and he had a temporary black-out. When he came-to he had lost height to about 16.000 ft. He then cut out the engine and circled over the sea. Finding that the engine would no longer work when he tried to cut it in again he picked the largest aerodrome he could see and glided down with wheels up.'

By the end of 1942 Malta was no longer under immediate threat, but the RAF remained in constant action, more often than not taking the fight to the enemy. Casualties in the air continued. On 6 May 1943 Flight Sergeant George Mercer (185 Squadron) baled out into the sea from where he was rescued by the crew of HSL 107 and brought safely to St Paul's Bay.

On 20 June 1943 His Majesty King George VI visited Malta. Here, King George, wearing Royal Navy Dress Whites, inspects a guard of honour after stepping ashore at Custom House, Grand Harbour.

(**Opposite, above**) In July 1943, two months after the German *Afrikakorps* had surrendered in Tunisia, Malta played a prominent role as Allied Headquarters and as a forward air base during Operation 'Husky' – the Allied invasion of Sicily. Italy capitulated soon afterwards, on 8 September 1943. Two days later Italian warships began to arrive under escort at Malta, the triumphant occasion prompting a delighted Admiral Sir Andrew Cunningham to signal the Admiralty: 'Be pleased to inform their Lordships that the Italian Battle Fleet now lies at anchor under the guns of the Fortress of Malta.' These are some of the surrendered ships at St Paul's Bay. American military personnel, complete with baseball bat, man the Bofors gun. Although American troops were not involved in the battle, they were present for a time on Malta and Gozo after the siege had been lifted.

(**Opposite, below**) Kingsway, also known as Strada Reale, before the Blitz, with the city's Opera House visible at centre-right. This impressive building, erected in the nineteenth century, was a city landmark.

(**Above, left**) Kingsway after the Luftwaffe had bombed the area.

(**Above, right**) Kingsway was later renamed Republic Street. The ruins of the Opera House were left as a reminder of the Second World War. In more recent years the site has been redeveloped as an open-air theatre.

Wartime destruction at Grand Harbour looking north-east towards Custom House, and the same view in more recent times from a window at Sptar Sir Paul Boffa.

It would be many years before Malta recovered from the devastation caused by Italian and German bombs. Damaged buildings were repaired, ruins demolished and bomb sites cleared. Even so, beach and defence posts and HAA gun emplacements remain. This is XHB 10, photographed at dusk stand-to in mid-1942 – and nearly 60 years later.

(**Above**) Malta was awarded the George Cross on 15 April 1942. But the island's ordeal was far from over and it was not until 13 September that a public presentation could at last be safely held. At Palace Square, Valletta, Lord Gort presented the George Cross to the Chief Justice, Sir George Borg, who received the award on behalf of the nation.

Palace Square in 1999. Today it is a pedestrian area.

Chapter Eight

Malta Today

After the end of the Second World War Malta continued to provide Britain with a military base until 1979. Pembroke served as the main barracks for land forces, both army and Royal Marines. Facilities were also maintained at Kalafrana, Safi and Qrendi. Ħal Far and Ta' Qali aerodromes were operational for years before they were eventually decommissioned. Luqa remained as the main RAF station. (A small civil airport was also established on the eastern edge of the wartime aerodrome.)

The site of RAF Luqa has since been expanded to incorporate the modern Malta International Airport, as well as the Air Wing of the Armed Forces of Malta (AFM). Ħal Far and Ta' Qali have both been redeveloped. Some former barracks were privatised. Pembroke is very different to what it was prior to the withdrawal of British Forces, while a shopping mall and apartments have replaced the old fortifications at Tigné. Manoel Island, which was heavily bombed, was left largely abandoned and derelict for decades, until a multi-million euro facelift began to transform the area.

Grand Harbour, the focus of so much attention during Italian and German air attacks, may from a distance appear much as it did before so many of its buildings were reduced to rubble. But a closer inspection of surviving original architecture will reveal the scars of countless bomb blasts. After 1945 Grand Harbour remained a regular port of call for the Royal Navy, and later hosted visiting warships of the Sixth Fleet of the United States Navy. Today, the port caters mainly for merchant ships and cruise liners.

Ħal Far Officers' Mess in 1942. The building was repaired and extended to include another floor. It was later taken over by the Employment and Training Corporation.

Former defence post HF5 at Ħal Far, after it was taken over as a farmhouse.

The remains of a machine gun found in a field close to HF5, where a Bf109 crashed with its pilot, Oberfeldwebel Otto Göthe (6./J.G.53), on 7 February 1942.

Air raid sirens. These are part of a curious collection of wartime artefacts gathered near the former aerodrome at Ħal Far by a local resident known as 'Pawlu Pete'.

A reminder of a bygone era at Wolseley Battery.

Discovered at Ta' Qali by the author in 1989, these Spitfire undercarriage doors were instrumental in initiating the rebuild of Spitfire EN199, now displayed at Malta's aviation museum.

Pictured in the autumn of 1989, Maltese Army Explosive Ordnance Disposal (EOD) personnel search for wartime UXBs in what is now agricultural land.

(**Left**) Near Dingli, in south Malta, skinning from a crashed Hurricane put to use as a field gate. Wartime repair of battle and/or shrapnel damage is clearly visible. (**Right**) Flying Officer John S. Southwell (261 Squadron) was shot down on 22 March 1941. Days later, his body was found on the north coast. His Hurricane may have crashed nearby, at Ras il-Qammieħ, from where these Hurricane remnants were recovered in the 1990s.

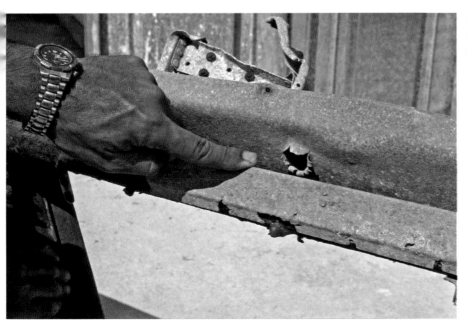

Bullet-holed Hurricane tail section retrieved from Ras il-Qammieħ.

Local farmers often made good use of items salvaged from crashed aircraft. In this case part of a Ju 88 has been utilised as a well cover. The aircraft flew into high ground on 18 January 1942, resulting in the loss of all three crew.

Pilot Officer Kenneth W. Pawson (601 Squadron) was shot down and killed on 25 April 1942. His Spitfire crashed just inland of Salina Bay, where this glycol header tank was discovered decades later.

American Pilot Officer Richard E. McHan (126 Squadron) survived after baling out of his Spitfire on 3 July 1942. The aircraft dived into a field near Siġġiewi, where both 20mm Hispano cannons became firmly lodged in bedrock. The bent barrel is believed to have resulted not from the crash but from efforts to remove the cannons.

A Spitfire aileron thought to have come from the crash site of Flying Officer A.I. (Ian) Lindsay (185 Squadron) who was shot down and killed on 23 October 1942.

RA6 (*left*), a typical wartime beach post, was built close to a seventeenth-century watchtower. This is where an Italian S.79 (*195ᵃ Squadriglia B.T.*) was shot down on 10 July 1940 – the first enemy aircraft to fall on Malta. All four crew died. Two occupants of RA6 who were severely burned died of their injuries two days later.

Grand Harbour, with Fort St Angelo (*middle left*) and Senglea (*middle right*).

In the summer of 1985 a joint British-Maltese operation was undertaken to clear wartime wreckage from Grand Harbour. Here, part of the hull of the merchantman *Talabot* is raised.

These are thought to be 4.7-inch guns from the destroyer HMS *Jersey*, sunk by a mine at the entrance to Grand Harbour on 2 May 1941.

(**Opposite, above**) Torpedoes recovered from the area where the destroyer HMS *Maori* was bombed and sunk in the early hours of 12 February 1942.

(**Opposite, below**) The author conducted several dives in December 2000 in an effort to locate aircraft wreckage on the seabed in Dockyard Creek. Poor visibility made a thorough search impossible, but this is believed to be part of a Ju 87 Stuka shot down on 10 May 1942.

(**Above**) A member of Malta's EOD diving team with a British aerial bomb just outside Grand Harbour.

The destroyer HMS *Kingston* was written off as a result of bombing attacks while at Malta Dockyard in April 1942 and was subsequently used as a blockship in the narrow channel between St Paul's Islands and the mainland. The wreck was later removed, but scattered fragments still litter the sandy seabed.

A Merlin engine recovered from the sea at Marsaskala and acquired by the aviation museum at Ta' Qali. It probably came from a Hurricane flown by American Pilot Officer James D. Tew (242 Squadron), who was killed on 1 March 1942.

Disused barracks at Għajn Tuffieħa. Feldwebel Rudolf Lenzner's Ju 88 (*9./L.G.1*) crashed on the ridge just behind the camp on 29 April 1941.

A beach post on Malta's northern coast close to where Sergente Maggiore Alberto Porcarelli (*151ª Squadriglia C.T.*) was shot down and killed on 2 July 1942; his MC.202 crashed in the vicinity of the building right of the road.

Manoel Island, with Fort Manoel (*centre*) and the former submarine base at Lazzaretto.

The former submarine base at Manoel Island.

View from inside a gun emplacement at Fort Tigné.

Bomb damage at Fort Tigné.

One of the better-preserved HAA gun sites is XHB 10 near Qrendi.

After the end of the Second World War ex-servicemen and women would revisit Malta. In May 1992, at what used to be part of RAF Luqa, former members of 4th HAA Regiment RA gather with the Master Gunner, General Sir Martin Baker Farndale (*front, with blazer*), after Stan Fraser (*third from left*) had organised the purchase, refurbishment and shipment to Malta of four 3.7-inch guns: a memorial to Malta's wartime gunners.